Contents

EASY MEALS FOR THE ON-THE-GO COOK

Slow Cooker Convenience

Chicken Fiesta Soup

MAKES 8 SERVINGS ■ 15 MINUTES PREP TIME

4	boneless skinless cooked chicken breasts, shredded
1	can (14½ ounces) stewed tomatoes, drained
2	cans (4 ounces each) chopped green chilies
1	can (28 ounces) enchilada sauce
1	can (14½ ounces) chicken broth
1	cup finely chopped onion
2	cloves garlic, minced
1	teaspoon ground cumin
1	teaspoon chili powder
¾	teaspoon pepper
1	teaspoon salt
¼	cup minced fresh cilantro
1	cup frozen whole kernel corn
1	yellow squash, diced
1	zucchini, diced
8	tostada shells, crumbled
8	ounces shredded Cheddar cheese

1. Combine chicken, tomatoes, chilies, enchilada sauce, broth, onions, garlic, cumin, chili powder, pepper, salt, cilantro, corn, squash and zucchini in **CROCK-POT®** slow cooker.

2. Cover and cook on LOW 8 hours. To serve, fill individual bowls with soup. Garnish with crumbled tostada shells and cheese.

Recipe from SHAROON SMITH, ELK GROVE, CA

Crock-Pot®
Stoneware Slow Cooker

Fall Beef & Beer Casserole

MAKES 4 TO 6 SERVINGS ■ 15 MINUTES PREP TIME

2	tablespoons oil
1½	pounds stewing beef, cut into 1-inch cubes
2	tablespoons all-purpose flour
1	cup beef stock
2	cups brown ale
1	cup water
1	onion, sliced
2	carrots, sliced
1	leek, sliced
2	celery stalks, sliced
1	cup sliced mushrooms
1	turnip, cubed
1	teaspoon mixed herbs

1. Heat oil in large skillet over medium-high heat. Cook meat until browned on all sides. Lower heat and add flour to skillet. Cook 2 minutes, stirring frequently. Gradually add stock, ale, and water; bring to boil. Transfer mixture to **CROCK-POT®** slow cooker. Add remaining ingredients. Cover and cook on LOW 8 to 10 hours or on HIGH 4 to 6 hours.

2. Serve with mashed potatoes, noodles or rice.

Recipe from JANE BRACKETT, BETHEL PARK, PA

Easy Beef Stew

MAKES 4 TO 6 SERVINGS ■ 10 MINUTES PREP TIME

2	pounds beef stew meat, cut into 1-inch cubes
1	can (4 ounces) mushrooms
1	envelope (1 ounce) dry onion soup mix
⅓	cup red or white wine
1	can (10 ounces) cream of mushroom soup

Combine all ingredients in **CROCK-POT®** slow cooker. Cover and cook on LOW 8 to 12 hours. Serve over hot cooked noodles.

Recipe from JOHN WIZIK, AKELEY, MN

Fall Beef & Beer Casserole

Crock Pot
Stoneware Slow Cooker

Best Asian-Style Ribs

MAKES 6 TO 8 SERVINGS ■ 10 TO 15 MINUTES PREP TIME

LOW: 6 TO 7 HOURS ■ **HIGH:** 3 TO 3½ HOURS

2	full racks baby back pork ribs, split into 3 sections each
6	ounces hoisin sauce
2	tablespoons minced fresh ginger
½	cup maraschino cherries
½	cup rice wine vinegar
	Water to cover
4	scallions, chopped

1. Combine ribs, hoisin sauce, ginger, cherries, vinegar and water in **CROCK-POT®** slow cooker. Cover and cook on LOW 6 to 7 hours or on HIGH 3 to 3½ hours or until pork is done.

2. Remove ribs. Thicken sauce; heat uncovered or cook in saucepan until consistency of barbecue sauce. Sprinkle with scallions. Serve ribs with extra sauce.

Recipe from JENNIS HEAL, LINCOLN, RI

"I wanted to try something more creative, with very simple ingredients as well as simple steps, and then let the Crock-Pot® slow cooker do the rest of the work!"

Crock-Pot®
Stoneware Slow Cooker

Like Grandma's Chicken 'N Dumplings

MAKES 4 SERVINGS ■ 10 MINUTES PREP TIME

2	cups cooked chicken
1	can (10¾ ounces) cream of mushroom soup
1	can (10¾ ounces) cream of chicken soup
2	soup cans water
4	teaspoons all-purpose flour
2	teaspoons chicken bouillon granules
½	teaspoon black pepper
1	can refrigerated buttermilk biscuits (8 biscuits)

Combine all ingredients, except biscuits, in **CROCK-POT®** slow cooker. Cut biscuits into quarters and gently stir into mixture. Cover and cook on LOW 4 to 6 hours.

Recipe from KAREN COUGHLIN, JACKSONVILLE, FL

German-Style Bratwurst with Sauerkraut & Apples

MAKES 6 TO 8 SERVINGS ■ 10 MINUTES PREP TIME

4	pounds bratwurst
2	pounds sauerkraut
6	apples, peeled and sliced thin
1	white onion, sliced thin
½	tablespoon caraway seeds
	Black pepper, to taste
5	bottles German-style beer

Add all ingredients to **CROCK-POT®** slow cooker. Cover and cook on LOW 4 to 6 hours or until apples and onions are soft.

Recipe from JENNIS HEAL, LINCOLN, RI

Like Grandma's
Chicken 'N Dumplings

Crock&Pot
Stoneware Slow Cooker

Granny's Apple Cidered Onion Soup with Gouda Cinnamon Toast

MAKES 6 SERVINGS ■ 15 MINUTES PREP TIME

LOW: 8 TO 10 HOURS

2	tablespoons olive oil
4	tablespoons butter, cubed, divided
4	medium to large onions, peeled and thinly sliced
2	medium Granny Smith apples, peeled, cored and chopped
4	cups chicken broth
1½	cups apple cider
2	tablespoons brandy (optional)
	Salt and freshly ground black pepper, to taste
6	slices French or Italian bread, cut about ½ inch thick
2	tablespoons sugar
½	teaspoon ground cinnamon
2	cups shredded Gouda cheese, preferably aged

1. Spoon oil over bottom of 4- to 6-quart **CROCK-POT®** slow cooker; add 2 tablespoons butter, distributing evenly. Add onions and apples. Cover and cook on LOW 8 to 10 hours or until onions are softened and caramelized.

2. Add broth, cider and brandy, if desired. Season with salt and black pepper. Cover and cook on HIGH about 1 hour or until hot.

3. While soup is heating, make Gouda Cinnamon Toast. Preheat broiler. Spread remaining 2 tablespoons softened butter on one side of bread slices. Combine sugar and cinnamon. Sprinkle evenly over buttered bread. Place bread on baking sheet and toast under broiler until golden brown.

4. Remove from oven; turn bread over and sprinkle untoasted side with Gouda cheese. Return to broiler until cheese melts, taking care not to burn.

5. To serve, ladle soup into bowls and float Gouda Cinnamon Toast on top of each serving, cheese side up. Serve immediately.

Recipe from JANICE ELDER, CHARLOTTE, NC

Cinnamon Candy Applesauce

MAKES 6 SERVINGS ■ 10 MINUTES PREP TIME

10   to 12 apples, peeled, cored and chopped
¾   cup hot cinnamon candies
½   cup apple juice *or* water

Combine apples, candies and apple juice in **CROCK-POT®** slow cooker. Cover and cook on LOW 7 to 8 hours or on HIGH 4 hours or until desired consistency. Serve warm or chilled.

Recipe from AMY GOULET, ACTON, MA

LOW: 7 TO 8 HOURS ■ **HIGH:** 4 HOURS

Fruit Ambrosia with Dumplings

MAKES 4 TO 6 SERVINGS ■ 20 MINUTES PREP TIME

LOW: 5 TO 6 HOURS ■ HIGH: 2½ TO 3 HOURS

4	cups fresh or frozen fruit*
½	cup plus 2 tablespoons granulated sugar, divided
½	cup warm apple or cran-apple juice
2	tablespoons quick-cooking tapioca
1	cup all-purpose flour
1¼	teaspoons baking powder
¼	teaspoon salt
3	tablespoons butter or margarine, cut into small pieces
½	cup milk
1	large egg
2	tablespoons brown sugar, plus additional for garnish
	Vanilla ice cream, whipped cream *or* fruity yogurt (optional)

*Use strawberries, raspberries, blueberries or peaches.

1. Combine fruit, ½ cup granulated sugar, juice and tapioca in **CROCK-POT®** slow cooker. Cover and cook on LOW 5 to 6 hours or on HIGH 2½ to 3 hours, or until fruit forms thick sauce.

2. Combine flour, 2 tablespoons granulated sugar, baking powder and salt in mixing bowl. Cut in butter using pastry cutter or 2 knives until mixture resembles coarse crumbs. Stir together milk and egg in small bowl. Pour milk and egg mixture into flour mixture. Stir until soft dough forms.

3. Turn **CROCK-POT®** slow cooker to HIGH. Drop dough by teaspoonfuls on top of fruit. Sprinkle dumplings with 2 tablespoons brown sugar. Cover and cook 30 minutes to 1 hour or until toothpick inserted in dumplings comes out clean.

4. Sprinkle dumplings with additional brown sugar, if desired. Serve warm. Garnish as desired.

Recipe from DIANE HALFERTY, CORPUS CHRISTI, TX

Spicy Cheese Soup

MAKES 6 TO 8 SERVINGS ■ 20 MINUTES PREP TIME

1   pound processed cheese, cubed
1   pound ground beef, cooked and drained
1   can (8¾ ounces) whole kernel corn, undrained
1   can (15 ounces) kidney beans, undrained
1   jalapeño pepper, seeded and diced* (optional)
1   can (14½ ounces) diced tomatoes with green chilies,
        undrained
1   can (14½ ounces) stewed tomatoes, undrained
1   envelope taco seasoning
     Corn chips (optional)

*Jalapeño peppers can sting and irritate the skin; wear rubber gloves when handling peppers and do not touch eyes. Wash hands after handling.

1. Combine cheese, beef, corn, beans, jalapeño, if desired, tomatoes, and taco seasoning in **CROCK-POT®** slow cooker.

2. Cover and cook on LOW 4 to 5 hours or on HIGH 3 hours. Serve with corn chips, if desired.

Recipe from KIMBERLY TAFLINGER, LIMA, OH

LOW: 4 TO 5 HOURS ■ **HIGH:** 3 HOURS

Vegetable-Overstuffed Pork Chops

MAKES 4 SERVINGS ■ 20 MINUTES PREP TIME

LOW: 4½ TO 5 HOURS

1	can (15¼ ounces) kernel corn, drained
1½	cups chopped green bell pepper
½	cup chopped yellow onion
1	cup HUNGRY JACK® Mashed Potatoes
½	cup uncooked long-grain converted rice
1	teaspoon dried oregano leaves
¾	teaspoon salt
⅛	teaspoon dried pepper flakes
4	thick pork chops, about 1 inch thick, trimmed of fat, split for stuffing*
	CRISCO® No-Stick Cooking Spray
½	teaspoon ground cumin
1	cup mild picante sauce
	Chopped cilantro, optional
1	medium lime, quartered, optional

Your butcher can cut a pocket in the sides of the pork chops to save time.

1. Combine corn, bell pepper, onion, HUNGRY JACK® Mashed Potatoes, rice, oregano, salt and pepper flakes in medium bowl. Toss to blend. Stuff each pork chop with about ½ cup vegetable mixture. Sprinkle with cumin.

2. Lightly coat **CROCK-POT®** slow cooker with Crisco® Cooking Spray. Place remaining vegetable mixture in **CROCK-POT®** slow cooker. Arrange pork chops in accordion-fashion on vegetable mixture. Pour picante sauce evenly over all. Cover and cook on LOW 4½ to 5 hours or until tender.

3. Remove chops from **CROCK-POT®** slow cooker and place on serving platter. Spoon vegetable mixture around chops and garnish with cilantro and lime juice, if desired.

Crock-Pot®
Stoneware Slow Cooker

Mama's Beer Chili

MAKES 4 TO 6 SERVINGS ■ 20 MINUTES PREP TIME

LOW: 8 TO 10 HOURS ■ HIGH: 4 TO 6 HOURS

2	tablespoons olive oil
1	large onion (Vidalia if available), diced
4	cloves garlic, crushed
1½	to 2 pounds ground turkey
1	can (28 ounces) crushed tomatoes
1	cup beer (dark preferred)
3	tablespoons chili powder
1	teaspoon curry
3	tablespoons hot sauce
⅓	cup honey
1	package (10 ounces) frozen corn
1	can (15 ounces) pink *or* kidney beans
⅓	cup diced mild green chilies
3	beef bouillon cubes
1	to 2 tablespoons flour, to thicken

1. Heat oil in large skillet over medium-low heat until hot. Add onion. Cook and stir 5 minutes. Add garlic; cook and stir 2 minutes.

2. Add turkey to skillet. Cook and stir until turkey is no longer pink. Drain fat and discard.

3. Add remaining ingredients, stirring until mixed. Transfer to **CROCK-POT®** slow cooker. Cover and cook on LOW 8 to 10 hours or on HIGH 4 to 6 hours.

Tip: Serve with corn bread and jam, or a loaf of fresh bread, if desired.

Recipe from SUE DENICE, RIDGEWOOD, NJ

Chicken Cacciatore

MAKES 4 SERVINGS ■ 10 MINUTES PREP TIME

LOW: 8 TO 10 HOURS ■ HIGH: 4 TO 6 HOURS

1½	**pounds boneless skinless chicken thighs**
1	**jar (1 pound 10 ounces) Ragú® Old World Style® Pasta Sauce**
1	**small green bell pepper, sliced**
1	**small onion, sliced**
3	**tablespoons dry sherry *or* chicken broth**
½	**teaspoon Lawry's® Garlic Powder With Parsley**
¼	**teaspoon ground black pepper**

1. Arrange chicken in **CROCK-POT®** slow cooker. Add pasta sauce, bell pepper, onion, sherry, garlic seasoning and black pepper.

2. Cover and cook on LOW for 8 to 10 hours or on HIGH for 4 to 6 hours or until chicken is thoroughly cooked. Serve, if desired, over hot cooked rice.

Crock·Pot®
Stoneware Slow Cooker

Harvest Time Turkey Loaf

MAKES 6 SERVINGS ■ 20 MINUTES PREP TIME

2	pounds ground turkey meat
2	beaten eggs
¾	cup bread crumbs
1	apple, peeled, cored and coarsely grated
¼	cup apple juice
¼	cup minced onion
½	cup shredded Cheddar cheese
¼	cup minced fresh parsley
¼	cup ground walnuts
½	teaspoon ground allspice
	Parsley sprigs and cranberry sauce (optional)

Combine all ingredients, except parsley sprigs and cranberry sauce, in large mixing bowl; mix well. Shape mixture into 7-inch round loaf. Place loaf in **CROCK-POT®** slow cooker. Cover and cook on LOW 5 to 6 hours. Slice turkey, and garnish with parsley and dollop of cranberry sauce, if desired.

Recipe from ROXANNE CHAN, ALBANY, CA

LOW: 5 TO 6 HOURS

Teriyaki Chicken Wings

MAKES 6 TO 8 SERVINGS ■ 10 MINUTES PREP TIME

3	to 4 pounds chicken wings
¼	cup soy sauce
¼	cup sherry
¼	cup honey
1	tablespoon hoisin sauce
1	tablespoon orange juice
2	cloves garlic, minced
1	red chili, minced (optional)

1. Place wings in **CROCK-POT®** slow cooker. Combine remaining ingredients in mixing bowl. Pour mixture over wings.

2. Cover and cook on LOW 3 to 3½ hours or on HIGH 1½ to 2 hours.

LOW: 3 TO 3½ HOURS
HIGH: 1½ TO 2 HOURS

Fire and Ice Chili

MAKES 10 SERVINGS ■ 25 MINUTES PREP TIME

1	can (20 ounces) DOLE® Pineapple Chunks
2	cans (14½ ounces each) diced tomatoes, undrained
1	can (6 ounces) tomato paste
1	can (4 ounces) diced green chiles
1	large DOLE® Yellow Onion, chopped (about 1½ cups)
1	DOLE® Green Bell Pepper, seeded, chopped
2	cloves garlic, finely chopped
3	tablespoons chili powder
4	teaspoons ground cumin
2	tablespoons finely chopped jalapeño chiles (optional)
1	teaspoon salt
½	teaspoon cayenne pepper
½	teaspoon hot red pepper flakes
1	tablespoon olive oil
3	pounds lean boneless pork butt, cut into 1-inch cubes
	Sliced green onions, shredded Cheddar cheese and sour cream (optional)

*Jalapeño peppers can sting and irritate the skin; wear rubber gloves when handling peppers and do not touch eyes. Wash hands after handling.

1. Drain pineapple chunks, reserve juice.

2. Combine reserved juice and tomatoes in a medium bowl with tomato paste, green chiles, onion, bell pepper, garlic, chili powder, cumin, jalapeño chiles, salt, cayenne pepper and pepper flakes.

3. Heat oil in Dutch oven or large saucepan. Brown meat on all sides in batches. (Don't overcrowd pot. Add just enough meat to cover bottom.)

4. Spoon browned pork into **CROCK-POT®** slow cooker; pour tomato mixture over pork. Cover and cook on LOW for 6 to 8 hours or on HIGH for 3 to 4 hours or until pork is tender.

5. Add pineapple chunks during last 30 minutes of cooking. Serve with green onions, cheese and sour cream, if desired.

Crock-Pot
Stoneware Slow Cooker

Heavenly Harvest Pork Roast

MAKES 6 TO 8 SERVINGS ■ 20 MINUTES PREP TIME

HIGH: 6 TO 8 HOURS

- ¼ **cup pomegranate juice**
- ¼ **cup sugar**
- 1 **tablespoon salt**
- 1 **teaspoon black pepper**
- 1 **tablespoon garlic salt**
- 1 **tablespoon steak seasoning**
- 1 **pork roast (4 to 5 pounds)**
- 2 **pears, cored, peeled and sliced thick**
- ½ **orange with peel, sliced thick**

1. Mix pomegranate juice and sugar together in small saucepan. Cook over low heat, stirring until sugar dissolves, about 2 minutes. Pour mixture into **CROCK-POT®** slow cooker.

2. Mix salt, pepper, garlic salt and steak seasoning together in small mixing bowl. Rub mixture over roast. Place roast in **CROCK-POT®** slow cooker. Turn roast to cover with juice. Top roast with pear and orange slices.

3. Cover and cook on HIGH 6 to 8 hours or until tender. Serve with juice and fruit slices.

Recipe from NANCI KISTLER, PLANO, TX

LESS TIME IN THE KITCHEN MEANS MORE TIME WITH YOUR GUESTS

Easy Entertaining

Triple Chocolate Fantasy

MAKES 36 SERVINGS ■ 20 MINUTES PREP TIME

HIGH: 1 HOUR PLUS 1 HOUR ON **LOW**

2   **pounds white almond bark, broken into pieces**
1   **bar (4 ounces) German chocolate, broken into pieces**
1   **package (12 ounces) semisweet chocolate chips**
3   **cups lightly toasted, coarsely chopped pecans**

1. Place chocolates in **CROCK-POT®** slow cooker. Cover and cook on HIGH for 1 hour. Do not stir.

2. Turn **CROCK-POT®** slow cooker to LOW. Continue cooking 1 hour, stirring every 15 minutes. Stir in nuts.

3. Drop mixture by tablespoonfuls onto baking sheet covered with waxed paper; let cool. Store in tightly covered container.

Recipe from DIANE HALFERTY, CORPUS CHRISTI, TX

Variations: Here are a few ideas for other imaginative add-ins:

- raisins
- chopped gum drops
- crushed peppermint candy
- chopped dried fruit
- candy-coated baking bits

- candied cherries
- crushed toffee
- chopped marshmallows
- peanuts or pistachios
- sweetened coconut

Harvest Bistro Pork Pot Roast

MAKES 6 TO 8 SERVINGS ■ 20 MINUTES PREP TIME

2   large onions, peeled and quartered
3   stalks celery, cut into 1- to 2-inch pieces
1   cup fresh whole cranberries
1   large pear, cored and cut into 8 wedges
1   large red cooking apple, cored and cut into 8 wedges
1   quince, peeled and chopped (optional)
2   tablespoons fresh thyme *or* 2 teaspoons dried thyme
⅔   cup packed dark brown sugar
2   teaspoons salt, divided
1   lean pork butt roast, cut into 2- to 3-inch pieces (about
       3 pounds)
1   cup chicken broth
6   to 8 ounces Brie cheese, chopped
       Fresh thyme (optional)

1. Combine onions, celery, cranberries, pear, apple and quince, if desired, in **CROCK-POT®** slow cooker. Sprinkle with thyme, sugar and 1 teaspoon salt. Place pork on top of mixture. Pour broth over pork. Sprinkle with ½ teaspoon salt. Cover and cook on LOW 7 hours.

2. Sprinkle cheese over pork. Cover and cook on LOW 1 hour. Transfer pork to serving platter. Arrange vegetables and fruit around pork. Taste and season with remaining salt, if needed. Garnish with additional fresh thyme, if desired.

Tip: Serve with cranberry relish or sauce, if desired.

Recipe from LEAH LYON, ADA, OK

Autumn Chicken

MAKES 10 TO 12 SERVINGS ■ 10 MINUTES PREP TIME

1	can (14 ounces) whole artichoke hearts, drained
1	can (14 ounces) whole mushrooms, halved
12	boneless skinless chicken breasts
1	jar (6½ ounces) marinated artichoke hearts, with liquid
¾	cup white wine
½	cup balsamic vinaigrette
	Hot cooked noodles
	Paprika for garnish (optional)

LOW: 4 TO 5 HOURS

1. Spread whole artichokes over bottom of **CROCK-POT®** slow cooker. Top with half of mushrooms. Layer chicken over mushrooms. Top chicken with marinated artichoke hearts with liquid. Add remaining mushrooms. Pour in wine and vinaigrette.

2. Cover and cook on LOW 4 to 5 hours.

3. Serve over hot cooked noodles. Garnish with paprika, if desired.

Recipe from JESSE MELTSNER, BLACKBURG, VA

Spicy Fruit Sauce

MAKES 4 TO 6 SERVINGS ■ 10 TO 15 MINUTES PREP TIME

¼   cup orange marmalade
¼   teaspoon pumpkin pie spice
1   can (6 ounces) frozen orange juice concentrate
2   cups canned pears, drained and diced
2   cups carambola (star fruit), sliced and seeds removed
    Pound cake slices (optional)
    Vanilla ice cream (optional)

1. Combine marmalade, pumpkin pie spice, orange juice concentrate, pears and carambola in **CROCK-POT®** slow cooker.

2. Cover and cook on LOW 4 to 6 hours or on HIGH 2 to 3 hours or until done. Serve warm over pound cake or ice cream, if desired.

Recipe from DIANE NEIBLING, OVERLAND PARK, KS

"I was looking for an easy way to make a
holiday dish that didn't have to go in the oven,
so I fixed the fruit sauce in the
Crock-Pot® slow cooker instead."

Ropa Vieja

MAKES 6 SERVINGS ■ **10 MINUTES PREP TIME**

LOW: 8 TO 10 HOURS ■ **HIGH:** 4 TO 6 HOURS

1	flank steak (1½ pounds)
	Salt and black pepper to taste
1	tablespoon olive oil
1	medium green bell pepper, chopped
1	jar (1 pound 10 ounces) Ragú® Chunky Pasta Sauce
½	cup beef broth *or* water
1	can (4 ounces) chopped green chilies, drained
¼	teaspoon red pepper flakes

1. Season steak with salt and pepper. Heat olive oil in skillet over medium-high heat. Cook steak for 3 to 4 minutes or until just browned.

2. Combine pasta sauce, green pepper, green chilies and red pepper flakes in **CROCK-POT®** slow cooker. Add flank steak, covering with sauce.

3. Cook on LOW for 8 to 10 hours or on HIGH for 4 to 6 hours or until meat is fork-tender. With 2 forks, shred meat. Return meat to sauce and heat through.

Tip: Ropa vieja translates to "old clothes," which the shredded meat in the recipe represents.

Crock⋆Pot®
Stoneware Slow Cooker

Fall-Off-the-Bone BBQ Ribs

MAKES 4 SERVINGS ■ 30 MINUTES PREP TIME

HIGH: 3½ HOURS

½	cup paprika
6	tablespoons sugar
¼	cup onion powder
1½	teaspoons salt
1½	teaspoons black pepper
2½	pounds pork baby back ribs, skinned
1	can (20 ounces) beer *or* beef stock
1	quart barbecue sauce
½	cup honey
	White sesame seeds (optional)
	Sliced chives (optional)

1. Lightly oil grill grate and preheat on HIGH.

2. While grill heats, combine paprika, sugar, onion powder, salt and pepper in large mixing bowl. Generously season ribs with dry rub mixture. Place ribs on grill. Cook 3 minutes on each side or until ribs have grill marks.

3. Portion ribs into sections of 3 to 4 bones. Place in 5-quart **CROCK-POT**® slow cooker. Pour beer over ribs. Cover and cook on HIGH 2 hours. Blend barbecue sauce and honey, and add to **CROCK-POT**® slow cooker. Cover and cook 1½ hours. Garnish with white sesame seeds and chives, if desired. Serve with extra sauce on the side.

Recipe from ADRIANNE CALVO, MIAMI, FL

Ragú's® Mediterranean Chicken

MAKES 6 SERVINGS ■ 10 MINUTES PREP TIME

LOW: 8 TO 10 HOURS ■ HIGH: 5 TO 6 HOURS

1	jar (1 pound 10 ounces) Ragú® Old World Style® Pasta Sauce
1	large onion, sliced
2	cloves garlic, minced
½	cup sliced pitted ripe olives
¼	cup dry white wine *or* chicken broth
.	Pinch ground cinnamon (optional)
1	chicken (3 to 4 pounds), cut into serving pieces
	Hot cooked rice (optional)
	Fresh rosemary (optional)

1. Combine pasta sauce, onion, garlic, olives, wine and cinnamon in **CROCK-POT®** slow cooker. Add chicken, coating with sauce.

2. Cook on LOW for 8 to 10 hours or on HIGH for 5 to 6 hours. Serve, over hot cooked rice and garnish with rosemary, if desired.

Try other Ragú® Pasta Sauces when preparing this dish, or substitute green olives, black oil-cured olives or kalamata olives in place of the sliced ripe black olives.

Scalloped Potatoes & Ham

HIGH: 3½ HOURS PLUS 1 HOUR ON LOW

- **6** large russet potatoes, sliced into ¼-inch rounds
- **1** ham steak (about 1½ pounds), cut into cubes
- **1** can (10¾ ounces) condensed cream of mushroom soup
- **1** soup can water
- **1** cup shredded Cheddar cheese
  Grill seasoning, to taste

1. Layer potatoes and ham in **CROCK-POT®** slow cooker.

2. Combine soup, water, cheese and seasoning in large mixing bowl. Pour mixture over potatoes and ham.

3. Cover and cook on HIGH 3½ hours until potatoes are fork-tender. Turn **CROCK-POT®** slow cooker to LOW and continue cooking 1 hour.

Recipe from CHRISTINA BRUNDICK, WINDSOR MILLS, MD

The Claus's Christmas Pudding

MAKES 12 SERVINGS ■ 30 TO 35 MINUTES PREP TIME

18	slices cranberry or other fruited bread
3	large egg yolks, beaten
1½	cups light cream
⅓	cup granulated sugar
¼	teaspoon kosher salt
1½	teaspoons cherry extract
⅔	cups sweetened dried cranberries
⅔	cup golden raisins
½	cup whole candied red cherries, halved
¾	cup plus 2 tablespoons cream sherry, divided
1	cup white chocolate baking chips
1	cup hot water
2	large egg yolks, beaten
¼	cup powdered sugar, sifted
¼	teaspoon vanilla
½	cup whipping cream

1. Preheat oven to 250°F. Place bread slices on baking sheet and bake 5 minutes. Turn and bake 5 minutes or until bread is dry.

2. For custard, combine 3 egg yolks, light cream, granulated sugar and salt in heavy saucepan. Cook and stir over medium heat until mixture coats metal spoon. Remove from heat. Set saucepan in sink of ice water to cool quickly. Stir 1 to 2 minutes. Stir in cherry extract. Cover surface with plastic wrap. Set aside.

3. Place cranberries and raisins in small bowl. Place cherries in another bowl. Heat ¾ cup sherry until warm. Pour sherry over cherries. Cut bread into ½-inch cubes. In large bowl, fold bread into custard until coated. Grease 6½-cup ceramic or glass bowl. Drain cherries, reserving sherry.

4. Arrange ¼ of cherries, plus ⅓ cup raisin mixture and ¼ cup baking chips in bottom of bowl. Add ¼ of bread cube mixture. Sprinkle with reserved sherry drained from cherries. Repeat layers 3 times, arranging fruit near edges of bowl. Pour remaining reserved sherry over all. Cover bowl tightly with foil.

5. Set bowl in **CROCK-POT®** slow cooker. Add hot water around bowl. Cover and cook on LOW 5½ hours. Unmold.

6. For sauce, combine 2 egg yolks, powdered sugar, 2 tablespoons sherry and vanilla. Beat whipping cream in small bowl until small peaks form. Fold whipped cream into egg yolk mixture. Cover and chill until serving time. Serve with warm pudding.

Recipe from DIANE HALFERTY, CORPUS CHRISTI, TX

Thai-Style Chicken Pumpkin Soup

MAKES 4 TO 6 SERVINGS ■ 15 MINUTES PREP TIME

LOW: 8 HOURS ■ HIGH: 4 HOURS

1	tablespoon extra-virgin olive oil
6	boneless skinless chicken breast halves, cut into 1-inch cubes
1	large white onion, peeled, halved and thinly sliced
3	cloves garlic, minced
1	tablespoon minced fresh ginger
½	to ¾ teaspoon crushed red pepper flakes
2	stalks celery, trimmed and diced
2	carrots, peeled, trimmed and diced
1	can (15 ounces) solid-pack pumpkin
½	cup mango nectar
½	cup fresh lime juice
½	cup creamy peanut butter
4	cups low-sodium chicken broth
3	tablespoons rice wine vinegar
½	cup minced fresh cilantro, divided
½	cup heavy cream
1	tablespoon cornstarch
2	to 4 cups hot cooked rice (preferably jasmine or basmati)
3	green onions, minced
½	cup roasted unsalted peanuts, coarsely chopped
	Lime wedges (optional)

1. Heat oil in large nonstick skillet over medium heat. Add chicken and cook, stirring occasionally, about 3 minutes. Add onion, garlic, ginger and red pepper flakes; cook 1 or 2 minutes longer or until mixture is fragrant. Remove from heat.

2. Place chicken mixture in **CROCK-POT®** slow cooker. Add celery, carrot, pumpkin, mango nectar, lime juice, peanut butter, broth and 2 cups water; stir to combine. Cover and cook on LOW 8 hours or on HIGH 4 hours.

3. Stir in vinegar and half of chopped cilantro. Mix cream and cornstarch together in small mixing bowl. Stir mixture into soup. If soup was cooked on LOW setting, turn setting to HIGH. Simmer, uncovered, 10 minutes or until soup thickens. To serve, put rice in soup bowls. Ladle soup around rice.

4. Sprinkle with remaining cilantro, green onions and peanuts. If desired, pass lime wedges for squeezing over soup.

Recipe from MARYBETH MANK, MESQUITE, TX

Meatball Hero Sandwiches

MAKES 4 SERVINGS ■ 10 MINUTES PREP TIME

LOW: 8 TO 10 HOURS ■ **HIGH:** 4 TO 6 HOURS

1	pound lean ground beef
1	egg
½	cup Italian seasoned dry bread crumbs
1	jar (1 pound 10 ounces) Ragú® Chunky Pasta Sauce
4	Italian rolls, (about 6 inches long each), halved lengthwise
1	cup shredded mozzarella cheese (about 4 ounces)

1. Combine ground beef, egg and bread crumbs in medium bowl. Shape mixture into 12 meatballs.

2. Arrange meatballs in **CROCK-POT®** slow cooker. Pour pasta sauce over meatballs.

3. Cook on LOW 8 to 10 hours or on HIGH 4 to 6 hours or until meatballs are done. Serve meatballs and sauce in rolls, topped with cheese.

Hot Beef Sandwiches au Jus

MAKES 8 TO 10 SERVINGS ■ 10 MINUTES PREP TIME

HIGH: 6 TO 8 HOURS

4	pounds beef rump roast
2	envelopes (1 ounce each) dried onion soup mix
2	teaspoons sugar
1	teaspoon oregano
1	tablespoon minced garlic
2	cans (10½ ounces each) beef broth
1	bottle (12 ounces) beer
	Crusty French rolls, sliced in half

1. Trim and discard excess fat from beef. Place beef in **CROCK-POT®** slow cooker.

2. Combine soup mix, sugar, oregano, garlic, broth and beer in large mixing bowl. Pour mixture over beef. Cover and cook on HIGH 6 to 8 hours or until beef is fork-tender.

3. Remove beef from **CROCK-POT®** slow cooker. Shred beef with 2 forks. Return beef to cooking liquid. Serve on crusty rolls with extra cooking liquid ("jus") on side for dipping.

Recipe from CAROLE ROSSMAN, MCCORDSVILLE, IN

Crock-Pot
Stoneware Slow Cooker

Big Al's Hot & Sweet Sausage Sandwich

MAKES 6 SERVINGS ■ 15 MINUTES PREP TIME

4 to 5 pounds hot Italian sausages
1 jar (26 ounces) spaghetti sauce
1 large onion, sliced (Vidalia preferred)
1 green bell pepper, cored, seeded and sliced
1 red bell pepper, cored, seeded and sliced
½ cup packed dark brown sugar
   Italian rolls, split open
   Provolone cheese, sliced (optional)

1. Combine sausages, spaghetti sauce, onion, bell peppers and sugar in 5-quart **CROCK-POT®** slow cooker. Cover and cook on LOW 8 to 10 hours or on HIGH 4 to 6 hours.

2. Place sausages on rolls. Top with vegetable mixture. Add provolone cheese, if desired.

Recipe from ALLYN TRANSUE, KITTANNING, PA

Warm Blue Crab Bruschetta

MAKES 16 SERVINGS ■ 30 MINUTES PREP TIME

4	cups peeled, seeded and diced Roma tomatoes
1	cup diced white onion
2	teaspoons minced garlic
⅓	cup olive oil
2	tablespoons balsamic vinegar
½	teaspoon dried oregano
2	tablespoons sugar
1	pound lump blue crabmeat, picked over for shells
1½	teaspoons kosher salt
½	teaspoon cracked black pepper
⅓	cup minced fresh basil
2	baguettes, sliced and toasted

LOW: 3 HOURS

1. Combine tomatoes, onion, garlic, oil, vinegar, oregano and sugar in **CROCK-POT®** slow cooker. Cover and cook on LOW 2 hours.

2. Add crab meat, salt and black pepper. Stir gently to mix, taking care not to break up crabmeat lumps. Cook on LOW 1 hour.

3. Fold in basil. Serve with toasted baguette slices.

Tip: Appetizer also can be served with Melba toast or whole-grain crackers.

Recipe from THOMAS LONG, NEW CUMBERLAND, PA

![Hunt's logo]

Family Fare

COMFORT FOOD TO SUIT EVERYONE'S TASTES

Homestyle Pot Roast

MAKES 6 SERVINGS ■ 10 MINUTES PREP TIME

2   pounds boneless beef chuck, cut into large chunks
1   can (14½ ounces) Hunt's® Stewed Tomatoes
1   packet (1½ ounces) beef stew seasoning

1. Combine beef, tomatoes and seasoning mix in **CROCK-POT®** slow cooker.

2. Cover and cook on LOW for 8 hours or on HIGH for 4 hours.

Great Idea!

Serve hearty Homestyle Pot Roast with boiled, halved new potatoes sprinkled with chopped parsley.

LOW: 8 HOURS ■ **HIGH:** 4 HOURS

Hunt's

Beef Stew

MAKES 6 SERVINGS ■ 20 MINUTES PREP TIME

1	medium onion, chopped (about ½ cup)
1	cup baby carrots
2	cups sliced celery
1	pound red potatoes, scrubbed and cubed
2	pounds beef stew meat, cut into chunks
2	teaspoons dried thyme leaves
1	can (14½ ounces) Hunt's® Diced Tomatoes in Juice
¾	cup water
1	can (6 ounces) Hunt's® Tomato Paste

1. Place onion evenly over the bottom of 3½-quart or larger **CROCK-POT®** slow cooker. Add the following ingredients in this order: carrots, celery, potatoes and beef. Sprinkle with thyme. Pour diced tomatoes and water over the top of beef.

2. Cover and cook on LOW for 8 to 10 hours until meat is tender. Stir in tomato paste; cover.

3. Cook 10 minutes.

Hunt's.

Hearty Beef & Bean Chili

MAKES 8 SERVINGS ■ 5 MINUTES PREP TIME

LOW: 8 TO 10 HOURS **HIGH:** 4 TO 6 HOURS

½ **pound boneless chuck roast, cut into large chunks**
1 **can (28 ounces) Hunt's® Whole Tomatoes**
1 **can (6 ounces) Hunt's® Tomato Paste**
1 **can (30 ounces) Hunt's® Chili Beans**
1 **packet (1¼ ounces) chili seasoning mix**

1. Combine roast, tomatoes, tomato paste, beans and seasoning mix in **CROCK-POT®** slow cooker.

2. Cover and cook on LOW for 8 to 10 hours or on HIGH for 4 to 6 hours.

Shredded Pork with Mushrooms

MAKES 8 SERVINGS ■ 10 MINUTES PREP TIME

LOW: 8 TO 10 HOURS **HIGH:** 4 TO 6 HOURS

3 **pounds boneless pork shoulder, cut into large chunks**
2 **cans (14½ ounces each) Hunt's® Stewed Tomatoes, undrained**
1 **can (6 ounces) Hunt's® Tomato Paste**
1 **packet (.87 ounce) pork gravy mix**
¼ **cup packed dark brown sugar**
1 **package (6 ounces) sliced fresh mushrooms**

1. Combine pork, tomatoes, tomato paste, gravy mix, sugar and mushrooms in **CROCK-POT®** slow cooker.

2. Cover and cook on LOW for 8 to 10 hours or on HIGH for 4 to 6 hours.

Hearty Beef & Bean Chili

Hunt's.

Italian Meatballs & Peppers

MAKES 8 SERVINGS ■ 10 MINUTES PREP TIME

LOW: 8 TO 10 HOURS **HIGH:** 4 TO 6 HOURS

2   cans (28 ounces each) Hunt's® Diced Tomatoes with Basil, Garlic & Oregano, undrained
1   can (6 ounces) Hunt's® Tomato Paste
1   pound frozen meatballs (about 32)
1   package (14 ounces) frozen pepper strips

1. Combine tomatoes, tomato paste, meatballs and pepper strips in **CROCK-POT®** slow cooker.

2. Cover and cook on LOW for 8 to 10 hours or on HIGH for 4 to 6 hours.

Creamy Tomato Potato Soup

MAKES 4 TO 6 SERVINGS ■ 5 MINUTES PREP TIME

LOW: 8 TO 10 HOURS **HIGH:** 4 TO 6 HOURS

1   package (11 ounces) creamy potato soup mix
2   cans (14½ ounces each) Hunt's® Petite Diced Tomatoes with Mild Green Chilies, undrained
4   cups water
1   pound small red potatoes, cut into quarters

1. Combine soup mix, tomatoes with chilies, water and potatoes in **CROCK-POT®** slow cooker.

2. Cover and cook on LOW for 8 to 10 hours or on HIGH for 4 to 6 hours.

Italian Meatballs & Peppers

Tomato Beef Stroganoff

MAKES 8 SERVINGS ■ 10 MINUTES PREP TIME

LOW: 8 TO 10 HOURS **HIGH:** 4 TO 6 HOURS

1   **boneless chuck roast (2½ pounds), cut into large chunks**
1   **can (28 ounces) Hunt's® Crushed Tomatoes**
1   **can (8 ounces) Hunt's® Tomato Sauce**
1   **can (6 ounces) Hunt's® Tomato Paste**
1   **package (6 ounces) sliced fresh mushrooms**
2   **packets (1½ ounces each) beef stroganoff seasoning**
2   **cups cooked noodles**
1   **cup sour cream**

1. Combine roast, tomatoes, tomato sauce, tomato paste, mushrooms and seasoning mix in **CROCK-POT®** slow cooker.

2. Cover and cook on LOW for 8 to 10 hours or on HIGH for 4 to 6 hours.

3. Add noodles to **CROCK-POT®** slow cooker the last 20 minutes of cooking.

4. Stir in sour cream at end of the cooking time.

Fiesta Chicken with Rice & Beans

MAKES 8 SERVINGS ■ 10 MINUTES PREP TIME

1 **can (15 ounces) Hunt's® Tomato Sauce**
2 **cans (14½ ounces each) Hunt's® Petite Diced Tomatoes with Green Chilies, undrained**
1 **cup long-grain rice**
1 **can (14½ ounces) Butterball® Chicken Broth**
1 **can (15 ounces) pinto beans, undrained**
1 **pound boneless skinless chicken thighs or breasts**
1 **packet (1 ounce) chicken taco seasoning**

1. Combine tomato sauce, tomatoes with chilies, rice, broth, beans, chicken and seasoning mix in **CROCK-POT®** slow cooker; stir to blend.

2. Cover and cook on LOW for 8 to 10 hours or on HIGH for 4 to 6 hours.

LOW: 8 TO 10 HOURS ■ **HIGH:** 4 TO 6 HOURS

Hunt's

Kettle Cooked Baked Beans with Smoked Sausage

MAKES 8 SERVINGS ■ 10 MINUTES PREP TIME

LOW: 4 TO 6 HOURS
HIGH: 2 TO 3 HOURS

1	package (3 ounces) Armour® Ready Crisp Fully Cooked Bacon, chopped
1	pound smoked sausage, sliced diagonally
1	medium onion, chopped (about ½ cup)
2	cans (31 ounces each) Van Camp's® Pork and Beans
1	can (6 ounces) Hunt's® Tomato Paste
½	cup Hunt's® Ketchup
¼	cup packed brown sugar
2	tablespoons Gulden's® Spicy Brown Mustard

1. Combine bacon, sausage, onion, beans, tomato paste, ketchup, sugar and mustard in **CROCK-POT®** slow cooker. Stir to blend.

2. Cook on LOW for 4 to 6 hours or on HIGH for 2 to 3 hours.

Savory Italian Sausage Stew

MAKES 8 SERVINGS ■ 10 MINUTES PREP TIME

LOW: 8 TO 10 HOURS
HIGH: 4 TO 6 HOURS

1¼	pounds mild Italian sausage, cut into 1-inch pieces
1	package (16 ounces) frozen Italian-style vegetables
2	medium zucchini, sliced
2	pounds round steak, cut into large chunks
1	can (26½ ounces) Hunt's® Four Cheese Spaghetti Sauce
1	can (28 ounces) Hunt's® Diced Tomatoes, undrained
1	can (6 ounces) Hunt's® Tomato Paste

1. Brown sausage in large skillet; drain.

2. Combine sausage, vegetables, zucchini, steak, spaghetti sauce, tomatoes and tomato paste in **CROCK-POT®** slow cooker. Stir to blend.

3. Cover and cook on LOW for 8 to 10 hours or HIGH for 4 to 6 hours.

Kettle Cooked Baked Beans
with Smoked Sausage

ENJOY GOURMET MEALS THAT ARE EASY TO PREPARE

Home Chef

Fall-Apart Pork Roast with Mole

MAKES 6 SERVINGS ■ 15 MINUTES PREP TIME

- ⅔ **cup whole almonds**
- ⅔ **cup raisins**
- 3 **tablespoons vegetable oil, divided**
- ½ **cup chopped onion**
- 4 **cloves garlic, chopped**
- 2¾ **pounds lean boneless pork shoulder roast, well trimmed**
- 1 **can (14½ ounces) diced fire-roasted tomatoes *or* diced tomatoes, undrained**
- 1 **cup cubed bread, any variety**
- ½ **cup chicken broth**
- 2 **ounces Mexican chocolate, chopped**
- 2 **tablespoons chipotle peppers in adobo sauce, chopped**
- 1 **teaspoon salt**
  Fresh cilantro, coarsely chopped (optional)

1. Heat large skillet over medium-high heat. Add almonds, and toast 3 to 4 minutes, stirring frequently, until fragrant. Add raisins. Cook 1 to 2 minutes longer, stirring constantly, until raisins begin to plump. Place half of almond mixture in large mixing bowl. Reserve remaining half for garnish.

2. In same skillet, heat 1 tablespoon oil. Add onions and garlic. Cook 2 to 3 minutes, stirring constantly, until softened. Add to almond mixture; set aside.

3. Heat remaining oil in same skillet. Add pork roast and brown on all sides, about 5 to 7 minutes. Place pork roast in **CROCK-POT®** slow cooker.

4. Combine tomatoes with juice, bread, broth, chocolate, chipotle peppers and salt with almond mixture. Process mixture in blender, in 2 or 3 batches, until smooth. Pour mixture over pork.

5. Cover and cook on LOW 7 to 8 hours or on HIGH 3 to 4 hours or until pork is done. Remove pork roast from **CROCK-POT®** slow cooker. Whisk sauce until smooth and spoon over roast. Garnish with reserved almond mixture and chopped cilantro, if desired.

Recipe from NANCY MAUER, BROOKLYN PARK, MN

Slow Cooker Cassoulet

MAKES 4 SERVINGS ■ 30 MINUTES PREP TIME

LOW: 8 HOURS

1	pound white beans, such as Great Northern
	Boiling water to cover beans
1	tablespoon butter
1	tablespoon canola oil
4	veal shanks, 1½ inches thick, tied for cooking
3	cups beef broth
4	ounces maple-smoked bacon *or* pancetta
3	cloves garlic, mashed
1	sprig each thyme and savory *or* a bouquet garni of 1 tablespoon each
2	whole cloves
	Salt and pepper, to taste
4	mild Italian sausages

1. Rinse and sort beans, and place in large bowl; cover completely with water. Soak 6 to 8 hours or overnight. (To quick-soak beans, place beans in large saucepan; cover with water. Bring to a boil over high heat. Boil 2 minutes. Remove from heat; let soak, covered 1 hour.) Drain beans; discard water.

2. Heat butter and oil in large skillet over medium-high heat until hot. Sear shanks on all sides until browned. Transfer to **CROCK-POT®** slow cooker. Add broth, bacon, garlic, beans, herbs, and cloves. Add enough water to cover beans, if needed. Cover and cook on LOW 8 hours. After about 4 hours, check liquid and add boiling water as needed.

3. Before serving, season with salt and pepper. Grill sausages; serve with cassoulet.

Recipe from **DIANE HALFERTY, CORPUS CHRISTI, TX**

Quatro Frijoles con Pollo Cantaro

MAKES 6 SERVINGS ■ 15 MINUTES PREP TIME

LOW: 4 TO 5 HOURS

1	cup ripe pitted black olives, drained
1	pound boneless skinless chicken breast*, cubed
1	can (16 ounces) garbanzo beans, rinsed and drained
1	can (16 ounces) Great Northern *or* navy beans, rinsed and drained
1	can (15 ounces) cannellini beans, rinsed and drained
1	can (16 ounces) red kidney beans, rinsed and drained
1	can (7 ounces) chopped mild green chilies, drained
2	cups chicken stock, plus extra as needed
2	tablespoons canola *or* olive oil
1	cup minced onions
2	teaspoons minced garlic
1½	teaspoons ground cumin
	Hot sauce, to taste
	Salt and black pepper, to taste
2	cups crushed corn chips
6	ounces Monterey Jack cheese, grated

*Turkey, pork or beef can be substituted for chicken.

1. Combine olives, chicken, beans, chilies and chicken stock in **CROCK-POT®** slow cooker. Mix well; set aside.

2. Heat oil in large skillet over medium-high heat. Cook onion, garlic and cumin until onions are soft, stirring frequently. Add to chicken mixture. Cover and cook on LOW 4 to 5 hours. Check liquid about halfway through, adding more hot broth as needed.

3. Taste and add hot sauce, salt and pepper. Serve in warm bowls and garnish with corn chips and cheese.

Recipe from DIANE HALFERTY, CORPUS CHRISTI, TX

Crock•Pot®
Stoneware Slow Cooker

Maple Whiskey Glazed Beef Brisket

MAKES 4 TO 6 SERVINGS ■ 20 MINUTES PREP TIME

LOW: 7 TO 9 HOURS

1	teaspoon ground red pepper
1	tablespoon coarse salt
½	teaspoon freshly ground black pepper
1½	to 2 pounds beef brisket, scored with a knife on both sides
2	tablespoons olive oil
½	cup maple syrup
¼	cup whiskey
2	tablespoons packed brown sugar
1	tablespoon tomato paste
	Juice of 1 orange
2	cloves of garlic, mashed
4	slices (¹⁄₁₆ inch thick each) fresh ginger
4	slices (½×1½ inches) orange peel

1. Combine red pepper, salt and black pepper in small mixing bowl. Rub over brisket. Place brisket in resealable plastic food storage bag. Set aside.

2. Combine oil, syrup, whiskey, sugar, tomato paste, orange juice, garlic, ginger and orange peel in mixing bowl. Stir to mix. Pour mixture over brisket in resealable storage bag.

3. Marinate brisket, refrigerated, at least 2 hours or overnight.

4. Transfer brisket and marinade to **CROCK-POT®** slow cooker. Cover and cook on LOW 7 to 9 hours, turning brisket once or twice. Adjust seasonings to taste. Slice thinly across the grain and serve.

Crock·Pot
Stoneware Slow Cooker

Jamaica-Me-Crazy Chicken Tropicale

MAKES 4 SERVINGS ■ 10 MINUTES PREP TIME

LOW: 7 TO 9 HOURS ■ HIGH: 3 TO 4 HOURS

2	medium sweet potatoes, peeled, cut into 2-inch pieces
1	can (8 ounces) water chestnuts, drained and sliced
1	cup golden raisins
1	can (20 ounces) pineapple tidbits in pineapple juice, drained and juice reserved
4	boneless skinless chicken breasts
4	teaspoons Jamaican jerk seasoning, or to taste
¼	cup dried onion flakes
3	tablespoons grated fresh ginger
2	tablespoons Worcestershire sauce
1	tablespoon grated lime peel
1	teaspoon cumin seed, slightly crushed
	Hot cooked rice

1. Place sweet potatoes in **CROCK-POT®** slow cooker. Add water chestnuts, raisins and pineapple tidbits; mix well.

2. Sprinkle chicken with jerk seasoning. Place chicken over potato mixture.

3. Combine reserved pineapple juice, onion flakes, ginger, Worcestershire sauce, lime peel and cumin seed in small bowl. Pour mixture over chicken. Cover and cook on on LOW 7 to 9 hours or on HIGH 3 to 4 hours, or until chicken and potatoes are fork-tender. Serve with rice, if desired.

Recipe from MARY LOUISE LEVER, ROME, GA

"I'm always looking for short-cuts, like using a slow cooker or canned pineapple in its own juice instead of fresh."

Meatballs with Sweet Orange-Chipotle Sauce

MAKES 8 SERVINGS ■ 25 MINUTES PREP TIME

1	can (15 ounces) diced tomatoes, drained
1	can (8 ounces) tomato sauce
¼	cup chopped onion
2	tablespoons tomato paste
¼	cup packed dark brown sugar
1	medium chipotle pepper in adobo sauce, finely chopped, about 1 tablespoon
1	teaspoon dried oregano leaves
1	teaspoon grated orange zest, divided
1	pound ground beef
½	cup HUNGRY JACK® Mashed Potatoes
1	large egg
3	tablespoons finely chopped fresh cilantro
2	cloves garlic, minced
¼	teaspoon salt
	CRISCO® No-Stick Cooking Spray
2	teaspoons Worcestershire sauce

1. Combine tomatoes, tomato sauce, onion, tomato paste, sugar, chipotle pepper, oregano and ½ teaspoon orange zest in **CROCK-POT®** slow cooker. Cover and cook on LOW for 4 hours.

2. Meanwhile, combine ground beef, HUNGRY JACK® Mashed Potatoes, egg, cilantro, garlic, remaining ½ teaspoon orange zest and salt. Roll mixture into 32 meatballs, each about 1 inch.

3. Lightly coat large nonstick skillet with Crisco® Cooking Spray. Cook meatballs in skillet over medium heat until well browned. Drain meatballs and reserve.

4. Add Worcestershire sauce and meatballs to **CROCK-POT®** slow cooker and stir. Cover and cook on LOW 30 minutes.

![Crock-Pot Stoneware Slow Cooker]

Portuguese Madeira Beef Shanks

MAKES 4 SERVINGS ■ 15 MINUTES PREP TIME

LOW: 7 TO 9 HOURS

4	cloves garlic, minced
1	large white onion, diced
1	bell pepper, cored and diced
2	jalapeño peppers, seeded and minced
½	cup diced celery
½	cup minced parsley
4	medium bone-in beef shanks (about 3 pounds total)
1	tablespoon minced fresh rosemary
1	teaspoon salt
1	cup beef broth
1	cup dry Madeira wine
4	cups hot steamed rice
	Horseradish sauce (optional)

1. Place garlic, onion, bell pepper, jalapeño peppers, celery and parsley in **CROCK-POT®** slow cooker.

2. Rub beef shanks with rosemary and salt. Place shanks on top of vegetables. Pour broth and wine over meat and vegetables. Cover and cook on LOW 7 to 9 hours. Taste and add more salt if needed.

3. To serve, spoon 1 cup rice into each soup plate. Top rice with beef shank. Spoon vegetable sauce over shanks. Offer horseradish sauce, if desired.

Recipe from FRANCES BENTHIN, SCIO, OR

Carne Rellenos

MAKES 6 SERVINGS ■ PREP TIME: 20 MINUTES

1	can (4 ounces) mild whole green chilies, drained
4	ounces cream cheese, softened
1	flank steak (about 2 pounds)
1½	cups salsa verde (green salsa)

1. Slit whole chilies open on one side with sharp knife; stuff with cream cheese.

2. Open steak flat on sheet of waxed paper. Score steak and turn over. Lay stuffed chilies across unscored side of steak. Roll up and tie with kitchen string.

3. Place steak in **CROCK-POT®** slow cooker. Pour in salsa. Cover and cook on LOW 6 to 8 hours or on HIGH 3 to 4 hours or until meat is fork-tender.

4. Remove steak and cut into 6 pieces. Serve with sauce.

Recipe from MICKEY STRANG, MCKINLEYVILLE, CA

LOW: 6 TO 8 HOURS ■ HIGH: 3 TO 4 HOURS

Mediterranean Chicken Breast and Wild Rice

LOW: 8 HOURS

MAKES 4 SERVINGS ■ 10 MINUTES PREP TIME

1 pound boneless skinless chicken breasts, lightly pounded
  Kosher salt, to taste
  Freshly ground black pepper, to taste
1 cup wild-rice blend
10 cloves garlic, mashed
½ cup oil-packed *or* dry sun-dried tomatoes*
½ cup capers, drained
2 cups water
½ cup fresh-squeezed lemon juice
¼ cup extra-virgin olive oil

*If using dry sun-dried tomatoes, soak in boiling water to soften before chopping.

1. Season chicken with salt and black pepper. Place chicken in **CROCK-POT®** slow cooker. Add rice, garlic, tomatoes and capers; stir well.

2. Mix water, lemon juice and oil in small mixing bowl. Pour mixture over rice and chicken. Stir once to coat. Cover and cook on LOW 8 hours.

Recipe from ADRIANNE CALVO, MIAMI, FL

Smoky Chipotle Cassoulet

MAKES 6 SERVINGS ■ 10 MINUTES PREP TIME

1	pound boneless skinless chicken thighs, cubed
1	teaspoon salt
1	teaspoon ground cumin
1	bay leaf
1	chipotle pepper in adobo sauce, minced
1	medium onion, diced
1	can (15 ounces) navy beans, rinsed and drained
1	can (15 ounces) black beans, rinsed and drained
1	can (14½ ounces) crushed tomatoes
1½	cups chicken stock
½	cup fresh-squeezed orange juice
¼	cup chopped fresh cilantro (optional)

1. Combine all ingredients, except cilantro, in **CROCK-POT®** slow cooker. Cover and cook on LOW 7 to 8 hours or on HIGH 4 to 5 hours..

2. Remove bay leaf before serving. Garnish with cilantro, if desired.

Recipe from LISA RENSHAW, KANSAS CITY, MO

LOW: 7 TO 8 HOURS ■ HIGH: 4 TO 5 HOURS

Crock Pot
Stoneware Slow Cooker

Linguiça & Green Bean Soup

MAKES 6 SERVINGS ■ 20 MINUTES PREP TIME

LOW: 8 TO 10 HOURS ■ HIGH: 4 TO 6 HOURS

1	large yellow onion, chopped
3	cloves garlic, minced
2	tablespoons olive oil
1	cup tomato juice
4	cups water
1	tablespoon Italian seasoning
2	teaspoons garlic salt
1	teaspoon ground cumin
1	bay leaf
2	cans (16 ounces each) cut green beans, drained
1	can (16 ounces) kidney beans, drained
1	pound fried linguiça sausage, cut into bite-sized pieces

1. Add all ingredients to **CROCK-POT®** slow cooker. Cover and cook on LOW 8 to 10 hours or on HIGH 4 to 6 hours. Add more boiling water during cooking, if necessary.

2. Serve with warm cornbread.

Recipe from SHERYL PIMENTEL, TRACY, CA

Royal Roundsteak

MAKES 6 SERVINGS ■ 20 MINUTES PREP TIME

HIGH: 6 TO 7 HOURS

1	to 2 pounds roundsteak *or* stew meat cubes
1	to 2 tablespoons oil
1	envelope (1 ounce) dry onion soup mix
2	cans cream of mushroom soup
	Hot cooked rice *or* cooked egg noodles

1. Trim roundsteak and cut into cubes. (Partially freeze meat for easier cutting.)

2. Heat oil in large skillet over medium-high heat. Brown meat on all sides.

3. Combine dry soup mix and canned soup in mixing bowl. Pour into **CROCK-POT®** slow cooker. Add browned meat. Cover and cook on HIGH 6 to 7 hours.

4. To serve, spoon over prepared rice or egg noodles.

Recipe from KIM JORGENSEN, ST. GEORGE, UT